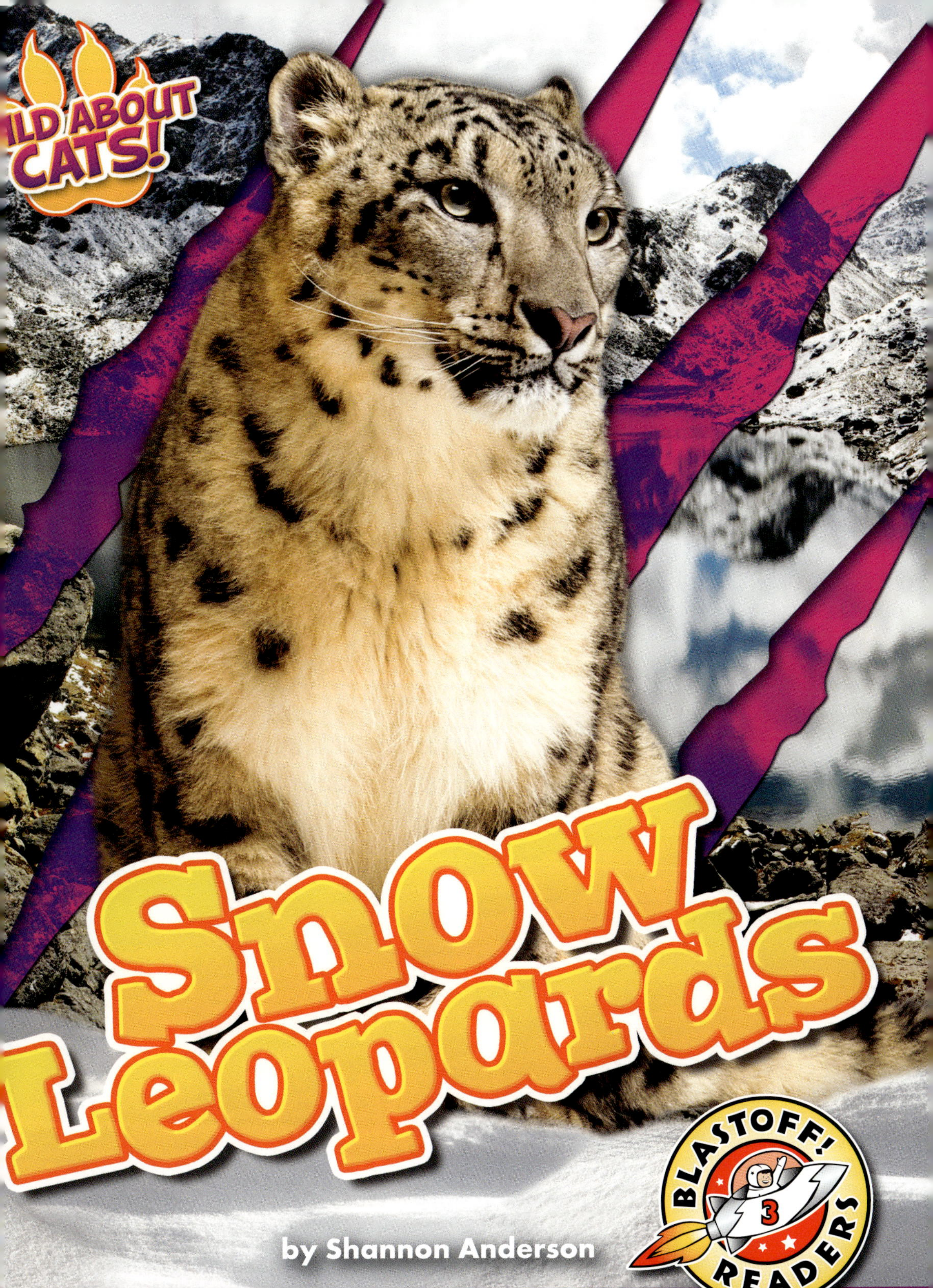

Snow Leopards

by Shannon Anderson

BELLWETHER MEDIA • MINNEAPOLIS, MN

Blastoff! Readers are carefully developed by literacy experts to build reading stamina and move students toward fluency by combining standards-based content with developmentally appropriate text.

Level 1 provides the most support through repetition of high-frequency words, light text, predictable sentence patterns, and strong visual support.

Level 2 offers early readers a bit more challenge through varied sentences, increased text load, and text-supportive special features.

Level 3 advances early-fluent readers toward fluency through increased text load, less reliance on photos, advancing concepts, longer sentences, and more complex special features.

★ Blastoff! Universe

This edition first published in 2025 by Bellwether Media, Inc.

Library of Congress Cataloging-in-Publication Data

LC record for Snow Leopards available at: https://lccn.loc.gov/2024046796

Editor: Suzane Nguyen Designer: Brittany McIntosh

Printed in the United States of America, North Mankato, MN.

Table of Contents

Ghost Cats 4
Built for Snow 8
Skillful Hunters 12
Leopard Litters 18
Glossary 22
To Learn More 23
Index 24

Ghost Cats

Snow leopards are sometimes called "ghosts of the mountains." They are hard to spot when they **camouflage** into rocks and snow.

They live and hunt high
in mountains and
in **shrublands**.

Snow leopards live in central and northern Asia.

Snow Leopard Range

Snow leopards are considered **vulnerable**. Their numbers are going down. People hunt them.

Built for Snow

Snow leopards are built for the cold and snow. Their thick, spotted fur keeps them warm.

Huge, furry paws help them walk on snow. Long, bushy tails help snow leopards balance when they climb.

Identify a Snow Leopard

Snow leopards are over 4 feet (1.2 meters) long. Their tails are around 3 feet (0.9 meters) long!

Size Comparison

house cat	snow leopard
height at shoulder	**height at shoulder**
around 10 inches (25 centimeters)	around 24 inches (61 centimeters)
length (without tail)	**length (without tail)**
around 18 inches (46 centimeters)	over 48 inches (122 centimeters)

Females weigh over 80 pounds (36 kilograms). Males weigh over 120 pounds (54 kilograms).

Skillful Hunters

Snow leopards are **solitary**. They mostly live and hunt in a home **territory**. Snow leopards stay away from one another. They mark their homes with pee.

Snow leopards mew, growl, and purr to **communicate**.

Snow leopards can hunt animals two to three times larger than them.

They **stalk** their **prey**. Then they **pounce**! They can jump as far as 50 feet (15 meters)!

Snow leopards are **carnivores**. Their favorite foods include ibex, marmots, and blue sheep. Sometimes they attack **livestock**.

The cats are slow eaters. They enjoy their meals over many days.

Snow Leopard Diet

Siberian ibex

Himalayan marmots

blue sheep

Leopard Litters

Snow leopard **litters** usually have one to five cubs. Mom raises the cubs on her own.

The cubs' eyes are closed during their first week. They can eat meat by two months old.

Baby Snow Leopards

name for babies: cubs
time with mom: about 18 months

Mom teaches the cubs to hunt. The cubs stay with mom until they are about 18 months old.

Then the cubs set off to explore the snowy mountains on their own!

In the Wild

habitats:

mountains

shrublands

conservation status: vulnerable

Least Concern	Near Threatened	Vulnerable	Endangered	Critically Endangered	Extinct in the Wild	Extinct

population in the wild: up to 5,000
population trend: going down
life span: up to 13 years

Glossary

camouflage—to use color in order to blend in with surroundings

carnivores—animals that only eat meat

communicate—to share information and feelings

litters—groups of babies that are born together

livestock—animals raised on a farm such as goats, sheep, and cows

pounce—to suddenly jump onto something

prey—animals that are hunted by other animals for food

shrublands—dry lands that have mostly low plants and few trees

solitary—living alone

stalk—to follow slowly and quietly

territory—the land area where an animal lives

vulnerable—at risk of becoming endangered

To Learn More

AT THE LIBRARY

Anderson, Shannon. *Clouded Leopards.* Minneapolis, Minn.: Bellwether Media, 2025.

Grack, Rachel. *Snow Leopards.* Minneapolis, Minn.: Bellwether Media, 2023.

Spilsbury, Louise. *Saving the Snow Leopard.* Bridgnorth, U.K.: Cheriton Children's Books, 2023.

ON THE WEB

FACTSURFER

Factsurfer.com gives you a safe, fun way to find more information.

1. Go to www.factsurfer.com.

2. Enter "snow leopards" into the search box and click 🔍.

3. Select your book cover to see a list of related content.

Index

Asia, 6
carnivores, 16
climb, 9
communicate, 13
cubs, 18, 19, 20
females, 11, 18, 20
foods, 16, 17, 19
fur, 8, 9
growl, 13
hunt, 5, 7, 12, 14, 20
identify, 9
in the wild, 21
jump, 15
litters, 18
males, 11
mew, 13
mountains, 4, 5, 20
name, 4
numbers, 7
paws, 9
pee, 12
pounce, 15
prey, 15, 16, 17
purr, 13
range, 6, 7
rocks, 4
shrublands, 5
size, 10, 11
size comparison, 11
snow, 4, 8, 9, 20
solitary, 12
stalk, 15
tails, 9, 10
territory, 12
vulnerable, 7

The images in this book are reproduced through the courtesy of: Eric Isselee, front cover (snow leopard), pp. 3, 9, 19 (left), 23; flocu, front cover (background); Don Johnston/ Alamy, p. 4; Srinivas Dumpati, p. 5; Mikhail Blajenov, p. 6; wesdotphotography/ Alamy, p. 8; Art-Y, p. 9 (inset); Dennis W Donohue, pp. 10-11; Nynke van Holten, p. 11 (house cat); clarst5, p. 11 (snow leopard); All Canada Photos/ Alamy, pp. 12, 14; Ondrej_Novotny_92, p. 13; Chris Desborough, p. 15; Tomas Hejlek, p. 16; Nature Picture Library/ Alamy, pp. 16-17; Yuriy Bartenev, p. 17 (Siberian ibex); Vladimir Melnik, p. 17 (Himalayan marmots); Steve Allen, p. 17 (blue sheep); blickwinkel/ Alamy, p. 18; Juniors Bildarchiv/ SuperStock, p. 19 (right); Evelyn Harrison/ Alamy, p. 20; Ondrej Prosicky, pp. 20-21.